Here's How to Deal

The Dance Dilemma

3 Docs Press

Shayna Brody Whitehouse, Ph.D.

Eleanor Gil-Kashiwabara, Psy.D.

Erika Qualls Laing, Psy.D.

Illustrations by Roberta Collier-Morales

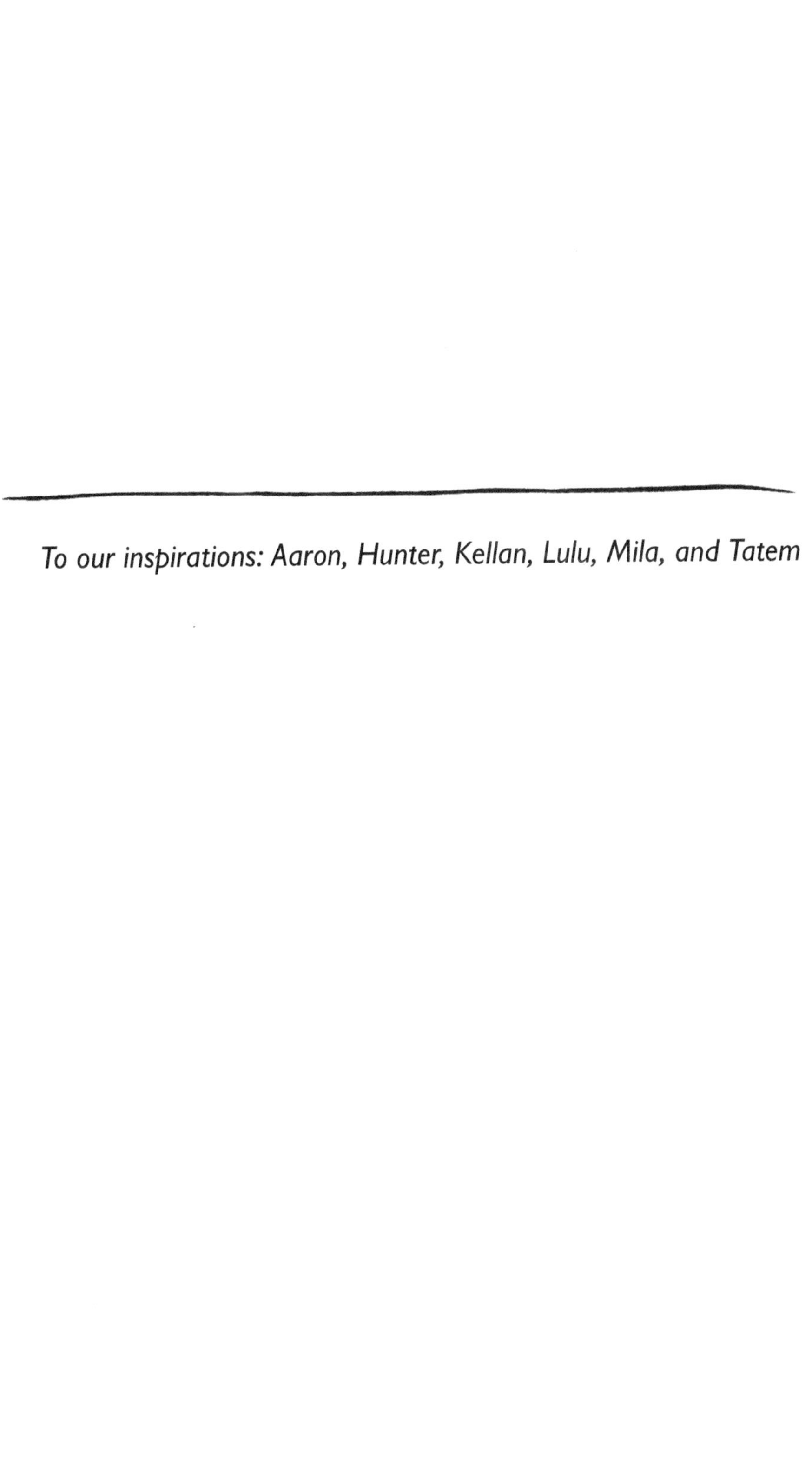

To our inspirations: Aaron, Hunter, Kellan, Lulu, Mila, and Tatem

Contents

About This Series

This is the first book in a series about kids figuring out How to Deal. In this story, the characters deal with friendships, honesty, bullying, and social media. Although concise, the content is meant as a tool for extensive discussion and thought. It is a resource to support sound emotional learning at home and in the school.

<u>Who</u>: This book is for kids and the people who care about them. This could be teachers, counselors, mentors, parents, and/or other adults.

<u>What</u>: Learning How to deal. Each particular book will address a variety of subjects. This could be about friends, teachers, school, family, feelings, and just about anything that might come up in life!

<u>When</u>: This can be read when questions come up for kids or proactively as a planned activity.

<u>Where</u>: This book can be read at school, at home, with friends, or just about anywhere.

<u>Why</u>: We are psychologists and parents that understand growing up can be hard, with big decisions and dilemmas that come up every day. We want to help kids learn to deal with those.

<u>How</u>: Within each chapter you will get a chance to explore the dilemmas each character faces and brainstorm ways to help them make good choices. You will follow each character for the same two weeks but from each of their perspectives. For example, you may hear about Monday from two different characters, so even though you know what happens you read about it from their point of view.

At the end of each chapter you will see this symbol, (?); that is your cue to go to the Companion Guide at the end of the book. The Companion Guide is organized with questions for events in each chapter. This is an opportunity to think about the issue in the story and how you might deal or feel in that situation.

1

Ben

Mold and Tests, Not a Winning Combo!

Monday

Ever had one of those days you just want to do over? That's me right now, and it's only 8:00 a.m. My name is Benjamin Allen Campbell, "Ben" for short, and I'm in 7th grade at North Morgan Middle School. I live in Lafayette, Oregon (I know you've probably never heard of the place) with my parents and younger brother. Why, you may ask, is the day already such a loss? Well, it's the first day back after Fall Break ... and the end of the last semester didn't go so well (as in not the best grades). Also, I just found out I've been moved to the seat next to my arch enemy since fifth grade, Penelope Whitaker. I'll explain later, but she is really annoying! This is my second year of middle school and even though most of the time I think it's okay, we have a lot more homework than last year. My best friends are Elías, Isaac, Alex, and Ashar. Elías and Isaac are in my homeroom – health with Ms. Rutherford. I wish we could sit next to each other, but I was moved early in the year for talking too much.

I get settled into my desk and am about to take out my binder when the crackle of the intercom makes me jump. It's Mr. Blakeman, our school principal, making morning announcements. Mostly what I hear is "blah, blah, blah, blah" but my ears perk up when Mr. Blakeman mentions that the Winter Snowflake Dance, affectionately called "The Flake," is only weeks away. I hope Ruby Monroe will be there. I've known her forever, but, since the beginning of the school year, it seems like things have changed. I feel weird every time I look at her and catch her looking back. I even think about whether she might want to go to the dance with me. Whoa! Like a date kind of thing!

In science class, we are assigned partners to work on our mold lab project. I hoped to be paired with Isaac or Elías, but they got paired with each other, and I got Randy Snodgrass. He picks ear wax out of his ear with a pencil. Yuck!

Tuesday

Elías and Isaac are really bugging me! At lunch today, they talk about the mold project, ditching me like I don't exist. I change the subject. "Hey guys, I got to the tenth level on Road Ninjas last night."

Elías perks up. "Really, dude? That's awesome. I'm still stuck at level 8. How'd you figure it out?" We spend the next ten minutes playing the game together. I feel part of the group again. While we focus on the game, I take a chance and ask the guys if they plan on going to The Flake. Mostly I just get shrugs, but Ashar says, "Why would you want to go to that dumb thing?"

"I don't know," I reply, "I think it could be fun. I heard Ruby and Josie talking about it. I wouldn't mind seeing Ruby, either." I don't plan on saying more but can't seem to shut my mouth. "She looks at me a lot ... which is kind of weird, but honestly, I kind of like looking at her, too."

Ashar groans, but then looks amused. "Sounds like you got a crush, dude!"

"Whatever," I say, "she's nice." Elías, who's been quiet the whole time, suddenly exits the game, throws his phone in his backpack and stomps out. I think what's bugging him? But shrug my shoulders. Whatever.

After lunch, Alex and I head outside to play basketball. He's a downer though. All he talks about are his parents' divorce and his older sister's cussing.

At the end of the day, Elías, Isaac, and I are at our lockers when the subject of the dance comes up again. Isaac asks Elías, "Are you going to ask anyone?"

Elías responds, "I know who I want to ask," but he won't say who. He screws up his face and kind of looks constipated. What is with him today?

I feel irritated when Mom picks me up and even more irritated when she says we have to go to the grocery store. Seriously? I want to play Road Ninjas! I don't tell her that or about Elías and Isaac getting to be mold lab partners, but I mutter and drag my feet so she can tell I'm in a bad mood. By the time we leave the store, I lose my computer time for having a "bad attitude." I mean, really, it's not fair! Today sucks!

Wednesday

I'm on my way to class when Isaac startles me, "Hey! Did you break level 10? What's 11 like?"

I tell Isaac with a proper amount of snottiness, "I didn't get to play Road Ninjas last night because I have a boot camp mom."

He says he understands, but if you ask me, I don't think he does. He does whatever he wants at home and all I have are rules and more rules and "consequences."

We talk about language arts and the fact that we have a big test on Friday. Now, that's something I'm not used to. Last year, we didn't have as many tests, mostly pop quizzes now and then. I didn't really need to study before, but it feels different this year. I also think language arts homework is harder, but I have to do it if I want to stay in the "advanced" class.

When I get home from school, I head out to ride my bike, but Mom calls from the front door, "Do you have any homework?"

I tell her, "I only have a few problems in math," but it's more like half a page. She gives me "the look" so I drop my bike at the front door and go in to do some of it. I tell her, again, I only have a few problems left and want to take advantage of the little daylight that's left. When I say, "My friends get free time when they get home," she frowns, crosses her arms, and taps her foot. She's a stickler for homework. It's not fair! I "finish," my homework (almost) and manage to get more Road Ninjas time, but it backfires when Mom realizes I still have more homework to do ... and it's 9:00. She's really steamed! I end up falling asleep with my face in my math book at my desk!

Thursday

I get to school and cram to get the rest of my math work done. It really is a bum deal. If everyone turns in their homework on time, we usually get free time on Fridays. It's not fair, if you ask me, to put all that pressure on us kids. I don't want to be responsible for everyone missing free time!

I see Ruby in choir before lunch. I've probably liked her since 3rd grade, but this year, it's different. She used to play Agent 66 with us guys, but, now, she only seems interested in her girl posse: Penelope, Marisol, and Josie. I say hi to her and am about to ask if she's going to the dance when Josie comes over, ignores me, and drags Ruby off by the elbow.

I'm tired after school and don't want to study for the language arts exam. I mean, how hard can it be? And to top it off, I am behind on the mold lab observations. Randy is giving me a hard time. I'm just done with this week—mold and tests are not a winning combo! I don't mention it to Mom.

Friday

I'm in BIG trouble. We started the language arts test and I am totally freaked out! The first few questions are fine, but I am seriously stumped on the others. I feel my face flush and I break into a cold sweat. This is going to be a major fail! I sit diagonally from Elías, and I've helped him before on homework, so now, maybe, he can help me. If I scoot forward half an inch I'll be able to see his paper. I know it's not honest, but if I mess this up, Mom is definitely going to take away my computer. Mrs. Finkelstein is texting behind her desk as usual. She'll never notice. I'm just going to slide forward a little bit.

(?)

2

Elías

To Flake or Flake Out

Monday

Ugh. That's all I can say.

After school, always the same routine. I get off the bus, goof around with my friends, head home, do homework, eat dinner, play football in the park, and head home to get ready for bed.

Fabian, my little brother, is playing Space Knights in the yard with the neighbor kid. He is so embarrassing, waving stuffed swords around at invisible flying dragons. When I walk inside, I hear the same question from my mom that I hear every day, *"¿Como es tu tarea, Elías?"* Homework. She always wants to know about homework.

Nothing different this afternoon. I tell my mom what I have for homework, but I make it sound like it's not real important. Today, I have other things on my mind.

Let me explain who I am. My name is Elías Muñoz and I am a 12-year-old seventh grader at North Morgan Middle School. We speak Spanglish, which is English mixed with Spanish, in my house. My mom teaches kids who are learning English at the elementary school, and she wants me to know both languages.

I try to grab a snack and head upstairs without having to talk more with my mom. I say "uh huh" to several more questions she fires my way and then go to my room. I pace back and forth between the desk and the bed. Luna, our cat, is curled up on the chair with her head popped up, watching me. I think I'm making her dizzy.

Ugh!! I do not feel like doing homework right now. I've got other problems. How am I supposed to think about writing the observations and predictions on the science mold lab? Let's just say the bread was soaked in water and then set in a Petri dish, and I predict it will get green, fuzzy, and gross. Isn't that enough?

Okay, the problem—just this morning the principal announced that the Winter Snowflake Dance is coming up, *rápido.* The Flake is a party with dancing, games, and cookies to mark the end of first semester. If I "Flake," I can go and hang with my friends. I know we will play the games and eat the cookies. That's not the problem. The problem is I really want to talk with Ruby. I see this as my moment. I have been thinking about this for a while now. The Flake! That is when I will talk to her.

I like her … I have liked her for two years. Isaac is the only one who knows. He can act goofy, like he's not paying attention, but he figured it out, and I swore him to secrecy. The last time I tried to talk to her, I was standing at my locker with Isaac, who was well aware of my long-time chicken-ness. He said, "Now's your chance. She's looking at you. Go say hi." I remember him pushing me towards her and, then, I dropped my books on the floor. I'm pretty sure I dropped them on purpose to avoid actually saying anything. Then, the bell rang and we had to run to math.

She is in some of my classes and we were in fourth grade together. She's cute, funny, and always with her friends. When she smiles, I swear the brown paint on the hallway walls turns a bright, happy yellow.

The Flake is a week from Friday and I don't know what to do. I weigh my options. Do I Flake or Flake Out?

1. I Flake: I wear my good jeans; put on the green shirt (my mom says green brings out the color of my eyes); bring some cookies; head to the game room; and hang with my friends. Then, I find Ruby and ask her if she is having fun. We fall into a great conversation. I wonder if I should hold her hand and lead her to the cookie table, maybe some games. In my vision, I am so smooth!

2. I Flake Out: *Or*, I won't be able to talk; I spit cookies at her while I try to talk; I trip on my feet. End up an outcast. I should stay home, eat cookies by myself, play video games with Fabian, and go to bed. Safe; no pressure; no friends pushing me to talk to her; no racing heart; and no sweating. No fear that words won't come out of my mouth. That sounds better. But, then there's no chance of being with Ruby.

What do I do? Maybe I should talk to Isaac.

My mom knocks on the door. I tell her to come in as I open the science notebook on my desk. She hands me a pile of laundry to put away. I hate to put that stuff away. I drop it on the ground and she looks at me with her *not-in-my-house* look. I sigh and grab the clothes. She is still standing there, looking at me. She says, *"Elías, ¿Que pasa?"*

I panic. What do I say? Do I tell her what's up? On one hand, she could probably give me good ideas. On the other hand, she'll think it's "cute" and will tell my dad, and I will be really embarrassed. I sit at my desk and stare at my science homework. *"Solo estoy haciendo mi tarea, Mama,"* I say, hoping she will believe I am focused on my homework. "Oh, and in 30 minutes, I'm meeting the guys to play football. Don't worry, no tackle."

"Okay ... *bueno*," she starts to walk out of the room.

That's when the words come spilling out of my mouth. "Hey what kind of cookies should I take to The Flake next Friday?"

She sits down on my bed and suggests chocolate chip. We talk about some of the games there might be, like a group scavenger hunt and limbo challenge. Then, I do it, like ripping off a bandage: "Mom, Isaac likes this girl and he doesn't know what to do. What can I ... or um ... he, say to this girl at The Flake? We're all trying to help him." I can't tell if she buys it or not. Long pause from my mom.

"I think he could bring her a cookie and ask if she would like it. That might get her to look at him. Then, if she takes it, he could ask how she likes The Flake and what games she's been playing. He could even ask if she wants to play one with him. I don't know if this would work for Isaac, but it might be an ice breaker ... *para romper el hielo.* Just a thought."

Okay, Mom actually has a good idea! I'm surprised. Then, she throws in that Isaac needs to shower before the dance so he smells good. Embarrassing! That's really uncalled for!

Tuesday

Lunch. It can be the best or the worst part of the day. It starts just fine. I sit with Isaac, Ben, and Ashar. We talk about the mold project and play *Road Ninjas.* That's when it happens. Ben, out of nowhere, starts talking about The Flake. I'm not really listening until he says, "I wouldn't mind seeing Ruby. She looks at me a lot." When he adds, "I kind of like looking at her, too," my stomach starts to flip flop.

What!?! I feel my face getting hot. I have to get out of here!

Ugh! Girls always like Ben. Of all the girls in the school, why does he have to like Ruby? I walk to the hallway, and Ms. Pierce,

the lunch lady, gets all official on me telling me I can't leave the room. Where the heck am I supposed to go? I need to cool down. I want to scream. How could *mi amigo* do that to me? I just helped Ben in language arts when the teacher asked him to answer a question he didn't hear because he was goofing off. I whispered the answer to him and he looked like a rock star! I am so done with that. I walk to the corner for a bit and stand there in disbelief. The eighth graders see me standing there like a dork. They start laughing and calling me a loser. I gotta get outta here. I sneak by the lunch lady and head to the bathroom where I stay in a stall until the bell rings.

It's time for mold. Ick! I hate this science lab. Mold growing on bread. It is so gross. Isaac is my lab partner ... he's my friend, but he can be immature sometimes. I try to measure the mold and see how much it grew over the last 24 hours. Isaac keeps talking about the mold as fuzzy boogers. He laughs without making a sound and snorts. He picks up the bread, hangs it from his pencil and pretends to dangle it from his nose. I look at him like—grow up! Ben, who is at the next table, looks over and sees him and starts laughing. It makes the science teacher look in our direction. Mr. Grossman yells, "Isaac and Elías! Put that down and get to work."

That does it; all the kids look at us. I see Ruby and her partner, Rebeccah, shake their heads in disgust. *Disgust!* She won't talk to me now. And I was not the one doing it! I was trying to go about my business, but no, I have to have an imma-ture lab partner. I *cannot* win today.

Thursday

Social studies. Mr. Rixby's class is a snooze fest. I sit next to Isaac, and he usually tries to distract me by making weird looks and funny noises. We start class by labeling our maps of WWII with battle sites. Mr. Rixby asks questions about the major events that brought the war to an end. I raise my hand to answer questions when no one else will. The clock hardly moves.

Then, Mr. Rixby asks Ruby a question. I see her jump in her seat and look at the teacher. Her mouth is open but nothing comes out.

Now's my chance! I quietly lean toward her and, tapping my mouth like I'm thinking, whisper the answer. I'd make *her* look like a rock star any time. She answers and Mr. Rixby moves on. Ruby turns toward me. I can feel my face get hot. She smiles at me! And, what do I do? Like a dork, I look down at my shoes. The bell rings and everyone jumps out of their seats. I do too, and all my books fall to the floor! Now I really look like an idiot. Ruby turns and smiles again. I think she's gonna laugh at me, but she bends down and helps me pick up my mess. Our hands touch. I mumble a thank you, and she says, "Elías, thanks for bailing me out!"

Suddenly, the moment is interrupted by Penelope yelling from the hallway, "Ruby, what's taking so long?" I watch Ruby leave. I'm in disbelief—she talked to me! I don't think I'll ever wash my hand again!

Friday

The big test! I studied for an hour last night. Shakespeare. I got this, no problem. I sit in my seat and Ben looks like he's trying to get my attention, but I shrug. I'm still bent out of shape that he wants to ask Ruby to the dance. I'm going to focus on this test. I'll deal with him later.

Mrs. Finkelstein passes out the test, tells us to start, and sits down, picking up her phone (whatever). The next thing I know, Mrs. F. says, "Elías and Ben. Come up here."

What just happened? I was writing my answers. I'm nervous as I walk up to her desk.

"Boys, you know cheating is against the code of conduct at this school. It is very serious."

What is she talking about? I'm sweating. I look at Ben and his face is bright red. Ben's cheating off me? What a jerk! I'm not taking the fall for this. He's on his own.

"Mrs. Finkelstein, I didn't cheat. I had no idea he was looking at my paper. I studied all last night." I can hardly breathe. What did he get me into?

She looks at Ben and says, "Mr. Campbell, is this true?"

Ben mumbles yes and shoots me a look. He wants me to help him! I'm not lying for him. Mrs. F. dismisses me, and I go back to my desk. I curl my arm around my paper and try to finish the test. I'm so mad, I can hardly focus.

(?)

3

Ruby

Distraction and Drama

Thursday

"Earth to Ms. Monroe, are you paying attention?"

I half jump in my seat and realize Mr. Rixby asked me a question. I have no idea what his question is, mostly because I'm thinking about earlier that day.

Before I go on, I should tell you who I am! My name is Ruby Monroe. I'm 13 years old and in seventh grade.

Anyway, something weird happened in choir, my favorite subject, probably the one thing I am good at and enjoy when it comes to school. I noticed Ben looking at me. Normally, that wouldn't be a big deal, but he's pretty much paid no attention to me since 6th grade. Before that, we were friends and even used to play *Agent 66* together. The fact that I looked up and saw him staring seemed kind of bizarre. Maybe I was singing off-key; maybe my bad-hair day was worse than I thought; or the concealer I *kind of* borrowed from my mom to cover my zit wore off. When the bell rang, he walked over to me and said "hi." He looked like he was about to say something else, but Josie came over and pulled me away. I wonder what he was going to say.

"Ms. Monroe? I'm still waiting for your answer."

I snap back to period 7 social studies but have no idea what Mr. Rixby asked. I open my mouth and start to panic when Elías whispers from behind me, "Germany."

I look up at Mr. Rixby and say with a shaky voice "Germany?"

"Thank you, Ms. Monroe, that is correct." He goes on teaching and I breathe a sigh of relief. I turn back toward Elías and smile my thanks. He really saved me on that one. I wish things came easier to me like they do for Elías. He's the smartest kid in our class.

The rest of class drags on for-EVER. I can't focus very well; probably my ADHD medicine is wearing off. When the bell finally rings, it startles me, and I hear a thump. Elías has dropped his books and papers on the floor so I help him pick them up. Our hands touch when we reach to gather the books. I feel embarrassed and self-conscious. Where is this coming from? I notice his dark hair and green eyes. He's kind of cute!

On the bus ride home, I sit with Penelope. She lives a few stops from mine in a super fancy neighborhood. Penelope's been one of my best friends since kindergarten. I like her except that she tries to tell me what to think sometimes. She's one of the more popular girls at school, but she's got a mean side. She used to be sweet and funny until everything changed a few years ago around the time her parents got divorced. I try to stay friends with her because I wouldn't want to be on her bad side.

I take a stupid chance and say to Penelope, "What do you think of Elías? He really helped me out today in social studies.

"That nerd? He can't even match his shirt and pants!"

"Oh," I say, "I guess you're right."

"Speaking of clothes," continues Penelope, "Ben always looks good. Plus, I think he's cute. I know I used to give him a hard time, but somehow, he's become really popular. I don't know why he hangs out with Elías; he doesn't need to."

"It's almost my stop," I say, "I'll catch you later!" I'm glad I don't have to continue the conversation. I'm feeling uncomfortable. Penelope just wants to talk about who's popular and what they wear.

Friday

Yay! Friday! My favorite day of the week. I drift off for a moment and think about the joy of the last period bell ringing later today. At that moment, my brain will stop hurting because it knows it will get a couple of days off from having to stay focused at school all day. I snap back to the here and now, where I am helping my little sister, Cali, get ready for school. Dad's still sleeping because he gets home late from his job as a volcanologist. He studies volcanoes. Pretty cool, huh?

My mom left an hour ago for her shift at Memorial General. She's been a nurse there for three years.

It's my job to help my sister get ready in the mornings, and, today, Cali fusses about wearing her jacket. It makes me mad! If she could get ready to go without causing a problem, my life would be easier. "Come on, we're going to miss our buses,"

I say and grab my backpack. At the last second, I look at the morning checklist my parents put on the fridge for me and I remember to take my ADHD medicine. Thank goodness for the checklist! If I had forgotten my medicine, I would have had a hard time focusing today. I turn my attention back to Cali, who is still whining as I pull her out the door to get her to her bus stop.

When I get to school, I head to my locker and Penelope walks up. "Dress yourself much?" she asks and pulls on the tag on my shirt. Oops, my shirt is inside out. As usual, Penelope looks great. Meanwhile, I feel like sinking into the floor. Before I

can comment or dash to the bathroom to flip my shirt around, she states, "I saw the conversation between you and Rebeccah last night."

Uh oh, where's this going? Is she talking about the conversation we had on our group text about The Flake and Rebeccah thinking Jason is cute? I think, sensing Penelope's mean streak.

"She's such a fail," continues Penelope. "I can't believe she wrote that she wants 'JT' to ask her to the dance! He's way out of her league! I'm going to tell Jason. I bet he needs a laugh!" Penelope shoves her locker shut.

Jason Thomas is the most popular 8th grader, and I'm worried. "Don't you think that's kind of mean? She actually didn't mean to tell the whole group and asked us to keep it quiet." I square my shoulders and try to look brave, but Penelope wins.

"Whatever," responds Penelope.

I hate it when she's mean like that. I like Rebeccah. I know I should stand up to Penelope, but I almost always chicken out. Trying to change the subject, I ask Penelope, "Who do you want to go to the dance with?"

Penelope gives me the *are-you-some-kind-of-idiot* look. "I'm not going WITH anyone. Daddy said he'll have his driver take us in his limo, so you and the girls have to go with me!"

That figures, I thought. *Once again we have to do what Penelope wants.* The bell rings and we leave in opposite directions. I hustle to the bathroom to fix my shirt before class.

I'm staring into space when Ms. Maxwell waves a paper in front of my face and thumps it on my desk. "Remember everyone, if you need extra help I have office hours on Tuesdays and Thursdays during lunch," she says. Even though Ms. Maxwell tells the class about her office hours, I just know she is directing her comment at me!

I look at my paper with the big red D circled. Great! I thought I did better on that test. I flip the paper over, hoping no one else saw it. I feel like crying and excuse myself to go to the bathroom.

Why is pre-algebra so difficult?! I can't keep track of all the parts of a problem! When I saw Dr. Stevens, she said the medicine should help all day, but I feel like I still can't do school! I feel so stupid! Dr. Stevens says I need to use "positive self-talk," but that's not helping either! I need to figure out how to focus in school and how to study so I remember everything for the tests. Yesterday, I lost my math homework so that will make my grade go down, too. Middle school is so overwhelming. I've tried to see Ms. Maxwell during office hours (when I actually remember to go), but that doesn't seem to help much either!

Okay, I have to get myself together to get back to class. *Deep breath, Ruby, you can do this.* After my break, I walk back to class, saying focus, focus, focus to myself. The bell! Yes, finally, going to choir.

I love this class. I can relax here.

After choir, I head to lunch, still singing in my head, and find my usual table. I put my tray next to Penelope. Marisol and Josie are already there. Penelope turns and whispers something to Marisol, who looks down and laughs.

I say, "What's so funny, guys?"

Marisol says, "Penelope said she told Jason about Rebeccah's text. I bet Jason got a laugh."

Penelope looks smug, and I'm not sure what to do or say. I feel sick. I hate this kind of drama.

At that moment, I see a group of boys walk to Rebeccah's table. They say something to her that I can't hear, but I do hear snickering and laughter. Rebeccah jumps up and runs out of the cafeteria. I look at Penelope, who is stifling a grin. My stomach sinks.

I get up and follow Rebeccah. When I open the bathroom door,

I hear sobbing in a stall. "Rebeccah, are you okay? It's me, Ruby."

"Go away!" Rebeccah responds. "I'm sure you knew Penelope was going to do this. How could you let her? I know she's your friend, but I thought you were my friend, too!"

"I am," I respond. "I'm so sorry that happened. Is there anything I can do to help?"

"You've *helped* enough," Rebeccah sobs. "You know I messed up by sending the group text. I asked everyone to keep it secret. You should have stood up for me. She actually listens to you! Just leave me alone!" At that moment, some other girls come into the restroom. I don't know what to do. I want to help, but I don't want to make things worse. Feeling confused, I leave the bathroom and go back to the table with the other girls. My stomach feels awful. Penelope is still laughing with Marisol and Josie about Rebeccah.

I turn around and look at the group of boys, and I see Jason and his buddies high-fiving. I look away and there's Elías. He's looking at me. We lock eyes for a second and, then, he turns away from me. I feel like total crap. Maybe I should just lock myself in one of the bathroom stalls for the rest of the day.

(?)

4

Penelope

Dressed to Impress

Thursday

Ugh, the bus. I hate that I have to take the bus. It always stinks like feet! I wish the boys would figure out they need to wear deodorant. Gross! Ruby's sitting next to me and I can tell she has something on her mind. "What do you think of Elías?" she says.

"That nerd? I say, "He can't even match his shirt and pants!" I tell Ruby that if I was going to be interested in anyone it would be Ben. He dresses nice and he's gotten to be one of the popular kids at school. I used to give him a hard time, but I've changed my mind about him. Daddy always says "It's not what you know, but who you know."

The bus comes to a stop and Ruby gets off. My stop is next. I hope Daddy will be home, but I can see from the car out front that it's my evil stepmom instead. Melinda and Daddy have been married for two years. Of course, they knew each other before my parents divorced. Oh, I'm sorry. Did I forget to introduce myself? My name is Penelope Whitaker, and I am 13 and in the seventh grade. I think most people would agree that I am the best-dressed girl at school and, honestly, the most popular.

I walk in and Melinda is doing some type of exercise in front of the TV. She barely glances at me. Fine, if she wants to pretend I don't exist, I'll do the same! I go up to my room and flop onto the bed. My pet bunny, Mr. Bun Bun, nibbles from his bowl. I look at him and flutter my eyelashes. "Mr. Bun Bun, what do you think? Is Mommy the prettiest girl you know? What? You think Ruby's nicer? No treat for you, Mr. Bun Bun!" I think about Ruby and how all the boys seem to like her.

I'm bored so I grab my phone and pull up my text messages. There is a group message that includes me, Ruby, Marisol, Josie, and two other girls that Ruby invited in, Rebeccah and Skylar. Those two are not really in our circle, and it's annoying that

Ruby added them. I don't know why she feels like she needs more friends when she has us! Whatever! I go along with it. They give me a laugh sometimes.

Eww, what's this text from Rebeccah? She and Ruby have apparently been chatting about the dance. Rebeccah says she hopes "JT" asks her to the dance. I know she's talking about Jason. He's pretty popular and probably never noticed Rebeccah. Rebeccah goes on about how "cute" he is. Why would he even consider asking her? She's such a do-gooder. Her parents wouldn't let her go with him anyway. They are so overprotective. I can't believe they go to every school event! Daddy hasn't gone to anything of mine this year. Like I care. He knows I'm not a baby anymore. I then see that Rebeccah only meant to text Ruby. Now she's asking us to keep it private ... as if! What an idiot. I am so annoyed and resist the urge to text something to Rebeccah about how ridiculous she is to think that JT would actually like her, but instead I hold back, thinking this could be a fun opportunity.

Friday

It's Friday morning, my favorite day of the week. Daddy always has his driver take me to school on Fridays. I put on my designer jeans and new jacket. I always lay out my clothes the night before. I feel pretty good about myself when I head downstairs. I see Daddy finishing his coffee. "Hi Daddy," I say.

"Are you dressed to impress, Princess?" he says. I smile, grab a bagel, and am about to grab the cream cheese when he adds. "Darling, do you really think you need that?" I feel my face turning red. "Don't you think you've gained a few pounds? You know, Melinda would let you do her exercise DVD with her."

"Okay, Daddy, I gotta go now," I say and run out the door feeling like I might burst into tears.

I get to school and see Ruby standing at her locker. I adore Ruby but what an airhead! She has her shirt on inside out. "Dress yourself much?" I pull the tag on the back of her shirt. I think, *why DO the boys like her? Her clothes always look thrown together.* I let Ruby know we are going to have some fun today with Rebeccah. I can't wait to see how dumb Rebeccah ends up looking. Ruby tries to be all sensitive and starts to tell me my idea is kind of mean but I brush her off. Whatever, she is just too nice sometimes! A moment later, Ruby asks about the dance and I tell her Daddy is letting us use his limo and driver and we will arrive in style. The bell rings before she can thank me.

I'm sitting in first period health. In front of me is Rebeccah, wearing that dorky headband with a bow attached. She's talking to Kayla about some trip she is taking with her parents this weekend. She is so stupid to be excited about it. I just want to rip that dumb headband off her head.

I raise my hand and ask to use the bathroom. This is going to be really funny to watch. I take a screenshot of her conversation with Ruby and send it as a text to Jason and his buddies. The headline reads "Rebeccah goody-good has a crush on you," then I write "LOL!" This is going to be great!

(?)

5

Ben

Truth and Consequences

Monday

I'm sitting in morning detention thinking how crummy my life is. Not only did I fail my language arts test, but I'm grounded and my best friend won't talk to me. I spent the weekend picking up Rambo's poop from the backyard, and my parents said, if I'm *lucky*, I'll get to go to the dance.

Speaking of my best friend, how could Elías throw me under the bus? He knows I helped him before. Yeah, sure, it was on homework, not a test, but I still helped him. Something's up with him anyway ... he's been acting weird since last week.

It's only four more days until "The Flake." If I'm going to ask

Ruby, it's now or never. After all, things can't get much worse! She's in choir with me just before lunch. That means I'll have a little extra time after the bell rings. I wish I could talk to Elías about this, but I don't think he will talk to me. Isaac's no help; he'll just make a joke. No matter what, though, I'm going to get up the guts to do it!

The morning seems to drag on. I see Elías briefly in the hall, but he avoids looking at me. We've been best friends for years but, could it really be over now? I slink into choir and scan the room. Ruby's in her seat, but she doesn't look happy. She's usually talking to someone. I wonder what's up. I start thinking about what I want to say to her. I like her, but I don't think she thinks of me that way. Through most of class, I rehearse what I will say to her. I'm so distracted I don't hear the bell ring.

Ruby is heading to the door, and I have to run to catch up or I'll lose my chance. I come up behind her and grab her shoulder, "Hey Ruby, do you have a minute?"

She looks around, startled, but then seems to relax when she sees it's me. "Ben, actually I wanted to talk to you too!"

Yes! I think, *maybe this won't be hard after all.* "You go first," I say.

Ruby takes a deep breath and says, "Well, it's kind of embarrassing, but we've been good friends for a long time."

My heart skips a beat. Could it be that she likes me, too?

Ruby continues, "I know you're good friends with Elías."

Elías? What? Where is she going with this?

"Well," says Ruby, "I'm worried he might be mad at me and ..." her voice trails off and she looks down at her shoes. Then, in almost a whisper, she says, "Would you ask him what he thinks of me?"

I'm stunned at this point. I realize she likes Elías! I can't believe it; she likes my best friend! Before I can stop myself, I blurt out, "Oh! You *like* Elías?"

Ruby glances up at me and says, "Well, yes, I kind of do like him. So, will you ask him?"

Before I know it, I say, "Uh, sure. Okay."

Ruby smiles, "Thanks, Ben, you're a good friend! Oh, and what did you want to talk to me about?"

I feel self-conscious and stupid, but I manage to hide it. "Oh, it's nothing," I mumble and fake a smile back at her.

I can't believe it! The girl I've been crushing on actually likes my best friend. I know Elías is likeable, but I don't think of him as someone that girls actually *like*. I work to pull myself together.

Tuesday

Morning detention, again. Three more days to go. *This blows.* I'm still trying to get my head around the fact that Ruby likes Elías. I guess it makes sense. He's smart and mostly a nice guy. Too bad, he still won't talk to me. Truthfully though, if I'm really honest with myself, I don't know if I would help Elías out if he tried to cheat off me either.

It's lunchtime and I'm running late. Everyone is at the table when I arrive. I sit down between Isaac and Ashar with Alex and Elías at the ends. Elías doesn't look at me. I wonder if the rest of the guys can tell something's up. I'm going to act normal, but, if Elías thinks I'm apologizing, he's going to be disappointed. I'm not ready yet.

The guys are talking about Rebeccah Berger and how she totally got burned by Penelope's crew. Isaac says he heard Penelope forwarded a text from Ruby to Jason about Rebeccah liking him, and Jason dissed Rebeccah to his buddies and anyone who would listen.

"It doesn't surprise me about Jason," I say. "He's a jerk. "I can't believe Ruby would go along with it though. That doesn't sound like her."

Elías jumps up and interjects, "Still, that's not how friends should treat each other." He looks at me with daggers in his eyes before he sits down, and I feel a tinge of guilt.

The guys notice our tension so Isaac starts talking about the mold project and how their mold is starting to look like Chewbacca from Star Wars. "Personally," says Ashar, "I think it looks like your face!" Both boys start laughing and exchanging insults. At least it's a distraction.

Last period; I can't wait for this day to be over. I see Elías walking ahead of me, but, suddenly, he stumbles. I notice Jason and his buddies walking behind him, laughing. I watch and see Jason step on the back of Elías' heels. Elías stumbles forward into the locker.

Jason is so lame. He's got his sights set on Elías. I act fast to close the gap to Jason. I act like I trip into Jason to distract him and say, "My bad!"

Jason calls me a loser and tells me to watch my back. Elías mumbles thanks and we both head out of school in different directions.

Wednesday

Here I am in detention again. Geez, I am so done with this. It's given me some time to think about my friendship with Elías though. We've been friends for so long, I'm not sure what school would be like if we aren't friends anymore. Probably boring. What should I have done during that test? I guess I could have studied—that's what my parents have been yelling at me for the past week. I should have taken the stupid test and dealt with the bad grade. I never had to really study before to get good grades. Maybe I'll talk with Elías. I guess it wasn't fair of me to cheat off him. I know he studies a lot to get his grades, and, maybe, I shouldn't have put him in that position.

Lunch ... running late again! Today's lunch is what I call "slop." They say it's healthy, but I can't tell what it is! Yuck! The menu describes it as "Natural Brown Rice with Chicken and Organic Broccoli." Looks like the lab mold made its way to the cafeteria today. What is "Natural Brown Rice" anyway? Is there non-natural brown rice?

I find the guys at the table. Elías is not here yet. I look around and see him still getting his food. We start talking about Road Ninjas. I tell the guys I haven't played this week. They joke and say, "Oh yeah, grounded, right?"

Elías comes to the table and sits next to me. "Hey," he says to me. "Thanks for having my back yesterday. I wasn't sure what else might have happened there."

"Sure," I say, "Jason really is a Class A jerk."

Elías goes on, "Sorry you're sitting in detention all week. Make any new friends?"

"It's alright," I say, "I deserved it. I put you in a bad spot and

I'm sorry about that."

Elías says, "Friends?"

I respond, "Yeah, dude." We do a knuckle bump and begin eating.

Isaac says, "Great! We are all friends again. Can we move on now?"

During recess, we play basketball. Just before the bell rings, I tell Elías about my conversation with Ruby.

He says, "But I thought you liked her."

"Yeah, I'm a little bummed," I say, pretending to be less disappointed than I really am. "But what am I going to do? She likes you."

At first, Elías seems happy with the news but, then, his face clouds over. "Thanks for letting me know." He shrugs.

That's weird. I thought he would be super excited. I wonder if it has to do with his comments at lunch yesterday and the whole thing with Rebeccah and Penelope.

(?)

6

Elías

Don't Flake on a Friendship

Monday

I am still upset about Ben and the test, and I am mad that Ben likes Ruby, too. I know he doesn't know I like her, but still. Although, after Friday, I'm not sure how much I like her anyway when she didn't stand up for her friend and stop Penelope. I don't know Rebeccah really well, but she seems pretty nice. Why would Ruby act like that? And why does she hang out with Penelope anyway? I thought Ruby was nicer than that.

"Elías, let's get going!" Mom's in a hurry again. "You'll be late for the bus, and I can't drive you in today." Luna sees me come down the hallway and backs into the pantry, meowing. I grab my waffle and bag and head out the door.

On the bus, I think about algebra. We get our results back from the qualification math test today. Mr. Ross said this test determines who goes to the State Math Competition - pretty cool. I am really excited about finding out how I did because I felt like I knew a lot of the answers. Last year, the group got to go to the beach after they took the State Test. They got to swim and relax in the sun while everyone else was stuck at school.

When I get to school, I pass Ruby in the hall. She looks like she wants to talk to me, but I'm not in the mood. I am still confused. I throw my stuff in my locker and head to homeroom health. A boring discussion follows on nutrition and reading food labels to make healthy decisions. I take my notes and leave class, avoiding Ben.

Next, algebra. I am looking forward to this! I really like algebra even though I am one of the only 7th graders in the 8th grade class. Math has always been easy for me. Mr. Ross is handing back our test papers and the suspense is building: did I make it? He hands me mine and says, "Great job, Muñoz, you'll be joining us at State."

Yessss!

I am still celebrating (inside) with a big old goofy grin (outside) when I hear Mr. Ross say to Jason, "Mr. Thomas, maybe you should take some lessons from Mr. Muñoz. This is below expectations."

Jason gives Mr. Ross a polite smile. "Thanks, Mr. Ross, I'll try harder next time." He turns toward me and, with gritted teeth, mumbles, "You'll pay for this, nerd!"

Great, just what I need—the older, more popular, and, did I mention huge 8th grader wants to kick my butt. I swear Jason flunked a grade. He's probably a foot taller than any of the other boys and plays quarterback on the football team. I make it through the day feeling a mix of excitement from the math test, disappointment from the stuff with Ruby and Ben, and a bit, no, a lot, of worry from Jason's comment.

Tuesday

At lunch, one of the guys mentions what happened with Rebeccah and how Penelope's crew treated her. Despite that I like Ruby, I still feel angry. I make the point that a good friend wouldn't act the way she did. I direct some of this toward Ben because, after all, he hasn't been a good friend, either.

I keep to myself as I sit down in social studies and start getting my books out. Ruby comes over to me and says, "Hi Elías. Can you help me with understanding the third question on here?" Even though I'm confused about Ruby right now, it's not like I wouldn't help her. We look at the question and I help her understand what the question is asking. She smiles and thanks me. I can't help but notice her cute dimples. I feel my face getting hot. Right then, Mr. Rixby starts class.

I'm ready for the day to be over when the bell rings, and I head to my locker. I feel someone push against me and I stumble. Then, I feel a shoe on my heel.

"Hey, dorkbot, I told you to watch your back!"

I catapult toward the lockers and have to regain my balance. Now, I'm scared. What the heck?

In a flash, I see Ben purposely launch himself toward Jason, which makes Jason stumble forward. "My bad," Ben says. Jason mutters something to Ben, and then he and his squad move on. Ben stops to ask if I'm okay.

"Thanks," I mumble. We head off in different directions. I'm not sure what to say.

On the bus ride home, I think about the day and what happened with Jason and how Ben helped. Despite how mad he made me last week, that was a pretty cool thing he did, defending me.

At home, I go upstairs and get out my homework. I have a hard time concentrating today. My books are open on my desk, but I am just staring at the words. I can't get anything done.

I'm quiet at dinner and Mom says *"¿Que piensas?"*

Sometimes I don't talk about silly friend things at home, but today is different. I have a lot on my mind. I tell her a little about Ben and the test and that I wonder how he could do that to a friend.

"Ah," she says, "I understand, *mi hijo*. Friendships are complicated. I can see why you're upset. Do you think he has been a good friend to you over the years? You have known each other a long time."

"That's true," I say. I think of how he helped me with homework in the past, all the fun things we've done, and how he helped me out today.

Dad adds, "It seems like you have been there for each other over the years."

"You know I think cheating is not right, but we learn right from wrong as we grow up. Overall, though, he usually is a good friend to you. Maybe being in detention all week helped him to learn this lesson. It is something to think about anyway." Mom concludes.

I take all that in and start feeling better, when Fabian pipes up. "I like Ben. He lets me play with you guys. This dessert is great!" We laugh because he has chocolate smeared across half his face. He says he wants to save the chocolate for later.

Wednesday

I slink into algebra hoping I can avoid eye-contact with Jason. He's already there, chatting with one of his squad. As I sit down, he says, "Hey, dweeb." He turns back to talk to his friend.

Whew! I don't think he's too interested today. But, I can tell I'm still on his radar. He never paid much attention to me before Monday, but I steer clear of him because he tends to look for a target. I keep my excitement about the State Math Competition to myself.

At lunch, I sit next to Ben and thank him for having my

back yesterday. He looks relieved and apologizes for the whole cheating thing. We both agree to move on, and I have to say I feel relieved. At recess, Ben tells me Ruby has a crush on me. On me! Wow, I can't believe it. She likes me over Ben! I am amazed, but I feel kind of guilty knowing that Ben likes her, too. Ben says he's bummed but okay with it. He is a good friend. Then I think about Ruby and the whole girl drama going on. It's deflating, and I feel confused. Ben notices and asks, "What's going on?" But, I tell him I don't want to talk about it. I've got to think this through.

After lunch, I sit in social studies, staring at Ruby's back. She tries to pass a note over to Rebeccah, dropping it on the floor and scooting it with her foot. Rebeccah shoves it right back to her. Ruby picks it up and crams it in her backpack as she slouches in her chair. As I watch, I think about what my mom said about everyone making mistakes and learning from them. I feel bad for Ruby that Rebeccah didn't accept the note. I think Ruby is really trying to be a good friend. I pass the time doodling a picture of a kid who looks suspiciously like Jason with a giant piano falling on him. I hope he's done with me.

Thursday

I'm at home doing homework and am distracted because I am thinking about the plans I made at school today with Ben, Isaac, Alex, and Ashar. We talked about meeting at Pizza Palace before the dance. I love pizza and am already drooling! After the dance, Alex is having us over for a sleepover. He has a cool air-hockey table at his house, but we hardly ever get invited anymore since his parents split. I look forward to that. I am glad Ben and I made up. He realizes he did something wrong, and I realize we all make mistakes.

I focus again on my homework and try to write up the new observations from today's mold lab. The bread is really getting gross. Now, I know why refrigeration is so important! I have a little left to write but once again, my thoughts drift to The Flake.

My mom knocks on the door and comes in, again, with laundry. Geez. I swear I have to put stuff away every day! She asks about my day and I tell her about the plans the guys and I made. She reminds me to use my manners at Alex's house. I give her the "duh" look. "I know that."

She smiles and says, "Hey, don't forget to remind Isaac

to use deodorant!" She winks and laughs as she walks out of the room. Luna walks in and meows as if she agrees with my mom. That is *so* not appropriate.

(?)

7

Ruby

Left Out and Limo-less

Monday

I tried to text Rebeccah this weekend, but I think she's blocked me. She won't respond either way. I still feel terrible about the whole situation. I was supposed to sleep over at Penelope's this weekend, but I made an excuse about not feeling well. I'm really upset with Penelope for what she did to Rebeccah, but I also feel like I should have stopped the whole thing. To be fair, I didn't know Penelope's exact plans, but I knew something not good was coming. Penelope has done this before. It makes me feel weird about our friendship, but we've been friends for so long and I don't want to be on her bad side. Am I afraid? I really don't know how to handle this. I feel bad and guilty about Rebeccah, but, to be honest, I feel bad for Penelope, too. I don't think she's happy at home. Her dad is a super busy guy; her stepmom ignores her; and she misses her mom.

When I get to school, I see Penelope at the lockers and she asks me if I still have "cooties." I shrug, tell her I'm feeling better, and run off to homeroom. On the way, I pass Elías in the hallway. We make eye contact and I smile. I'm about to say "hi" when he turns away and keeps walking. I'm worried he hates me after what happened on Friday. I really don't know what to do.

In choir, we practice for our recital. I notice Ben across the room and think about how we have always gotten along. I decide that, maybe, I'll talk to him about Elías.

At the end of class, I try to think of how to approach Ben when he comes up and asks if I have a minute. Perfect! I tell him I want to talk to him, too. He seems happy to talk to me and tells me to go first. I explain that I really like Elías, but I'm afraid I messed it up. He looks uncomfortable. I hope he's not mad at me, too. But, he says he'll talk to Elías for me. I ask what he wanted to talk to me about, but he says he has to get something before lunch.

The morning moves slowly and lunch is uncomfortable. I sit with Penelope and the others, but I don't say much. I keep feeling weird about everything. I look at Elías across the room, and he doesn't look at me. I hope Ben can help. Rebeccah is with two of her friends, Kayla and Skyler. They are both super academic, like Rebeccah. They sit close to her like they are protecting her. I sit quietly through lunch, which isn't hard because Penelope is leaving me out of the conversation.

Science lab is awkward today. Rebeccah and I are supposed to be working on our mold project together, but she avoids me and does her own thing. She measures the new growth and writes down answers without sharing. Every time I try to talk to her, she ignores me. Finally, I give up and start working on discussion questions, but I can't focus. I feel a little angry and that surprises me. After all, it wasn't me who embarrassed her. And she was the one who accidentally texted the group about her crush!

Later, in social studies, I still can't concentrate. I worry about the whole Rebeccah thing; I wonder if Elías still likes me; and I'm mad at Penelope. It's also frustrating that, even though I take my medicine, it doesn't seem to help. We have until Friday to complete a short-answer essay test on WWII. There are eight questions and I only have one done. I start to work on question 2 but am distracted by the pencil sharpener, kids laughing in the hall, and Barry Winstrom's snorty laugh.

Everything seems stressful today. I am glad when it is over.

Tuesday

The day drones on. I'm upset and I can't focus. I get to science lab early and see Rebeccah talking to Mr. Grossman. I can't hear what she says, but manage to hear Mr. Grossman when he says, "Rebeccah, you know we don't change lab partners. You have to make it work. It's only a little longer; then work with someone different on the next project."

My stomach sinks. She doesn't want to be my lab partner anymore! I run off before she can see me, try to collect myself and get back to class when the bell rings, all the while holding back tears.

By the time I get to social studies, I'm exhausted. I answered question 3 on our short-answer essay but don't think it's right. I see Elías and get up the guts to ask him for help. He seems happy to help me, which is a bright spot in the day. It's interesting that, when Elías explains something to me, it makes sense.

Wednesday

I decide to write Rebeccah an apology letter. I chat with Josie and Marisol at lunch. They are excited about riding in Penelope's limo for the dance. Funny, Penelope hasn't mentioned that to me again. I'm not sure I want to go with her anyway. I leave when Penelope arrives for lunch and find a spot in the library to write my letter. If I get to class early, I can hand it to Rebeccah.

Darn it! I'm running late to social studies and can't get there early. Class has begun when I drop the note on the floor and scoot it toward Rebeccah with my foot. She pushes it back to me. Wow! She won't read my letter. How am I going to fix this if she won't let me try?

That evening, I feel really down and Mom asks me what's up. I tell her what happened with Penelope and Rebeccah last week. I can tell by her face she's concerned. She asks a lot of different questions that make me think: "Why do you think you should apologize and how should you apologize?" I also ask her about friendships and what to do when you have a friend who makes a choice you don't agree with and might hurt another friend. We talk about what it means to be a friend and the importance of standing up for each other. I say, "I knew I should have stood up for Rebeccah but I didn't know how." She doesn't give me the answers, but it makes me think.

"Ugh, why is this friendship thing so hard?" I'm still thinking about my talk with mom after she leaves the room.

Thursday

I see Marisol and Josie at the lockers. Marisol looks sheepish and says, "I'm sorry about The Flake. I really wanted us all to go together. I don't know what Penelope's problem is."

I'm surprised because I didn't know I was excluded until now. But at the same time, I'm not surprised and respond, "That's okay. It's not your fault. I know how Penelope can be." I do feel disappointed, but I don't tell the girls. Josie makes a joke to lighten the mood. We are laughing when Penelope walks up.

(?)

8

Penelope

Perfect Dress

Sunday

This weekend was lame. Ruby was supposed to spend the night on Saturday but cancelled and said she was "sick." I can't help thinking it had something to do with Rebeccah and Friday.

I look at Mr. Bun Bun, "It was hilarious, Mr. Bun Bun. You should have seen Rebeccah's face when Jason and his pals showed her the text I copied. She deserves it, that goody-goody." Mr. Bun Bun gives me a blank look and twitches his ear. I take that as agreement. I think more about Ruby and my feeling that she's mad about the whole thing. I don't understand why she cares about Rebeccah anyway. It's not like Rebeccah is popular or can do anything for her. Maybe she just likes to copy off her in class. The more I think about it, the more irritated at Ruby I get. I hate to admit it, but the idea of her being angry at me or not being my friend is scary. Sometimes it's easier just to be mad.

Daddy knocks on the door to say he and Melinda are going to the Robinsons' garden party. "Can I go?" I ask.

"No dear," he says, "it's only for adults. Here's some money if you want to go to a movie. I'm sure Mr. Rivers could take you."

"Thanks Daddy," I say.

He adds, "But don't forget, you need to focus on your math homework. You know that's not your strong suit." He shuts the door, and I flop on my bed.

I look at Mr. Bun Bun, who is distracted by a carrot. "Nobody cares about me," I tell him and bury my head in the pillow. I feel like a loser.

Tuesday

I talk to Josie and Marisol about my fabulous weekend when Ruby walks up. I tell the girls that Ruby missed out because she had the cooties. Ruby doesn't respond. Am I taking this too far?

Whatever!

I get to health early and quickly copy the homework notes I got from Josie. In class, I daydream about The Flake on Friday but am also preoccupied with how Ruby is acting. I don't know if I'll invite her on the limo ride or not. It depends on if she starts being a better friend. I always trusted Ruby as a valued member of my group. After all, we've been best friends since kindergarten.

Wednesday

Before class, Josie, Marisol, and I talk about The Flake and taking Daddy's limo. The girls are really excited to arrive in style!

Josie says, "I can't wait for the four of us to pull up and look fab."

"Who said anything about *four* of us?" I say.

The girls give each other a look. "Remember this is invite only!"

Josie looks like she wants to say something but doesn't. The bell rings.

"Sorry, gotta go!" I say.

Later, at lunch, Ruby walks off when I arrive. Obviously, she is still stuck on the Rebeccah thing. That's it! She is not going with us Friday!

Thursday

At our lockers, Ruby, Marisol, and Josie are talking and laughing about something. I interrupt them, asking what they are wearing to The Flake. I confirm to Josie and Marisol that I'll pick them up with the limo at 6:30. I don't say a word to Ruby and pretend she's not there. The girls look at each other but remain silent. We change the subject to various gossip from that week, and Ruby makes some lame excuse and walks away. Good, that's what she gets for not being a good friend. So, why am I not more excited?

When I get off the bus that afternoon, I hope Dad is home. Of course, he is not. Melinda is doing yoga in the living room and ignores me. I go to my room and plop on my bed.

Why do I feel like crying right now? I look over at Mr. Bun Bun and notice the picture on the wall behind him of Ruby and me from dance class when we were eight. We have our arms around each other with big smiles. I was a lot happier then, and we were really good friends. Why is this so complicated? I feel alone. Dad is always working, and I'm a bother for Melinda. I wish I could FaceTime Mom, but she's out of town. I'm not supposed to call her unless it's an emergency. I don't think this qualifies.

I take Mr. Bun Bun out of his cage and give him some cuddles. "What should I do, Mr. Bun Bun? You know Ruby and I have been good friends. I can usually count on her. Why is this time different? Why does she care about Rebeccah, and why do I feel like I did something wrong?" Mr. Bun Bun looks at me and scrunches his nose. I put him back in the cage and decide to distract myself by picking out my clothes for The Flake. Daddy bought me the perfect dress!

(?)

Friday Flake Frenzy

Ben

Last day of detention. Yes! I am done with this. Today is going to be a good day. I can feel it. I'm excited for The Flake. I told Elías I'm fine if he asks Ruby to go, but he said he wants us guys to go together. We decided to stop at The Pizza Palace before the dance. After The Flake, Alex is having us all over to spend the night and my parents are letting me go! They said I did my time for the crime. I'm not doing that again!

I see Ruby in choir, "Hey," I say, "I put in a good word for you with Elías. Maybe you guys can talk at The Flake."

Ruby looks downcast, "I doubt it. I don't think I'm going to go."

"What do you mean," I say, "I thought you were going to arrive in style in Penelope's fancy limo?" I don't know if it's just me, but Ruby looks a little red-faced.

"Actually, Penelope didn't invite me and I wouldn't have wanted to anyway."

I can tell she doesn't want to say more so I don't push it.

Ms. Morgan, the choir teacher, clears her throat and sends daggers at us with her stare. "I shouldn't hear any talking right now. I know everyone is excited for the dance tonight, but we have to get ready for our recital."

Ruby and I both direct our attention to the front of the room, and our conversation ends. I feel bad for Ruby even though I don't understand how she's been friends with Penelope anyway.

After all, I have reasons I call her my "arch enemy." When I was in 5th grade, our class was studying meal-worm metamorphosis. It was silent in the room while we wrote down our observations. I was nudging my mealworm in the container, thinking he was probably dead, when a sharp loud noise that sounded suspiciously like a fart echoed through the room. Heads looked up and turned to where Penelope was sitting. She shrieks, "Gross Ben, can't you hold that in? Didn't your mom teach you manners?" The whole class burst out laughing. I felt my cheeks get red. I was stunned into silence and didn't defend myself. Mr. Schwartz tells the class to settle down, but the damage is done. For the rest of the week (and even for the few months after), at lunchtime, kids walked past me making farting noises. Nobody believed I was framed!

I come back to the present as the bell rings. Time for lunch!

Elías

The morning drags on; I can't stop thinking about the dance tonight. I walk into algebra and find my seat. I am getting out my books when I hear from behind me, "Morning, dork."

I ignore Jason and think, *Hurry up and start class, Mr. Ross.* Jason makes me nervous, but I remind myself, it's not my issue, it's his. I've been picked on before, and I know that bullies usually feel bad about themselves. I hate being the target. I try not to let him know it bugs me because that will make it worse. My heart is racing with panic, but I keep staring toward the front of the class. I decide to think about Ruby, and I still feel confused about her. She is trying to make up with Rebeccah. I don't know why she went along with Penelope and didn't stand up for Rebeccah.

In my book, Penelope is a bully, just like Jason.

Despite all this, I am looking forward to The Flake and maybe seeing Ruby tonight. I thought about asking her to go with me or even meet me there, but I heard she is going with Penelope.

Class moves on, and I don't feel Jason staring at me anymore. The few of us going to the State Math Competition have to stay to talk to Mr. Ross before lunch. It is going to be so cool! It's at the beach again this year and in a fancy hotel. I can't wait. I'm hoping for a beach day.

I hurry to lunch and see the guys already sitting at the table. I head toward them with my food. On the way, I pass Ruby, who is standing and talking loudly with Penelope. She is half yelling, "That wasn't nice, Penelope! Sorry, I'm passing on your limo."

What just happened? I am now more confused than I was. I go to sit down at the table and Ashar says, "Did you just hear Ruby tell off Penelope?"

"Yeah," I say. "What was that all about?"

Ashar replies, "I don't know, but I think it has something to do with Rebeccah. Who knows ... these girls and their drama." He sighs, shakes his head and then changes the subject, "Did you guys see the new upgrade on *Road Ninjas*? Maybe we can play that tonight at Alex's."

I am half listening to what they say about *Road Ninjas*, but I'm distracted by what just happened and think I may have been wrong about Ruby. I look over and see she's looking upset. She heads to Rebeccah's table and sits down to talk to her. I think I may have misjudged her. She is really trying to be a good friend. I turn and tell Ben what happened.

Later that day, I see Ben at the lockers. He smiles and says, "Hey, you owe me one. I invited Ruby to pizza. See you tonight!"

Ruby

I am so disorganized this morning! I have to get Cali ready and me ready, but I can't keep my mind on things. I keep thinking about Rebeccah being hurt and humiliated and that she won't talk to me. And, I also think about Penelope and how she is excluding me.

"Cali, come on and get your coat! We have to go!" We rush out of the house barely making our buses. As I finally sit down in the bus, I realize I forgot my medicine! That is going to make today harder. I look around and feel some relief that Penelope is not there. She must be getting a ride from her father's chauffeur today. That gives me some time to take deep breaths before I get to school.

I decided not to go to the dance tonight. I try to convince myself I shouldn't be upset about it—it's not a big deal.

The morning drags on. I'm in a bad mood and, on top of it, I can't concentrate. In choir, Ben asks me if I am going to The Flake. He seems excited about it, but I just say no. I think about what my mom and I talked about with apologies and friendships, and I really want to talk to Rebeccah. I don't know if I have the right words to say, but I have to talk to her face to face.

I walk into the cafeteria determined to make things right. Before I can get to Rebeccah's table, however, Marisol intercepts me. "Ruby, Penelope wants to talk to you." She grabs me by the elbow, ushering me to the table.

Penelope looks smug. "So, I've decided to invite you to come with us tonight. I don't know what your problem has been this week, but I'm willing to forgive you."

Seriously! She's forgiving me? I admit I've always been a little intimidated by Penelope, and we've been friends so long I've accepted how she is, but this is too much!

"Penelope, I know you don't really care, but I'm going to

tell you anyway. In fact, I should have stopped you before it all happened, but it was wrong what you did to Rebeccah. I know you thought you were being funny when you embarrassed her, but you weren't. That wasn't nice, Penelope! Sorry, but I'm passing on your limo." I walk away from the table.

I'm determined now to speak to Rebeccah and head to her table. I tap on her shoulder and ask if we can talk.

"Why bother?" she says.

I say, "Look Rebeccah, I know you're mad at me and you have a right to be. What Penelope did was wrong," I sit next to

her, "but I could have stopped it."

Rebeccah looks at me, unsure. "Well, I'm a little surprised to hear you say that. Aren't you one of Penelope's minions? I heard you're going to the dance tonight in her 'limo'."

"Actually, I'm not," I say. I sigh and go on, "She did invite me, but I'm not going with her. I really do feel bad for what happened. You're my friend, and I should have stood up for you. I'm sorry."

Rebeccah shrugs and seems to be thinking about what I just said to her. "Thanks for letting me know," she says and turns back to her lunch. She adds with a little smile, "I'll see you in social studies."

I feel better, I apologized to her face to face. I know it will take time for her to trust me again. At least, this is a start. Now I can eat. My stomach is not in knots anymore.

I run into Ben at the lockers and he says, "Hey, me and the guys are going to Pizza Palace before The Flake. Want to come? We can all go to the dance together then."

I am startled and respond, "Oh, okay. I'll think about it." Maybe today is getting better. I'm still not sure I want to go to the dance, but pizza might be okay.

Later in social studies, I'm thinking about what Ben said when Rebeccah comes in. She gives me a tentative smile and finds a seat. I have an idea. Maybe Rebeccah would want to meet for pizza with us and then we can go to The Flake together. Social studies drones on, and I watch the clock. The moment the bell rings, I say, "Hey Rebeccah! I have an idea. Ben and the guys invited me to meet them for pizza before The Flake tonight. Want to come with me? I'd really like you to."

Rebeccah pauses and says, "I'm not going to The Flake tonight. I don't want to be around those people and have them laugh at me."

I feel guilty, but I'm not giving up. "How about we just do pizza then?"

"Well," She considers, "I guess that would be ok."

"Great!" I say, "I'll pick you up!"

Penelope

Mr. Rivers is waiting for me at the car this morning. He opens the door. I get in and sit down. He says, "I am looking forward to taking you and your friends to the dance tonight. How many should I expect, Ms. Whitaker?"

I almost say four, but then remember I haven't invited Ruby. "I'm not sure." As I sit in silence on the ride to school, I begin to feel irritated. Ruby should feel lucky to be my friend. I am going to give her a chance to come in the limo with us to the dance. If she says no, then good riddance! I feel better about myself when I arrive at school. Why was I feeling bad in the first place?

When Mr. Rivers drops me off, I walk to where Josie and Marisol wait. I turn and point. "That's the car we will be in tonight, girls! By the way, Ruby's coming, too."

They smile and Josie says, "Did you ask her?"

"Well, I will at lunch, but she'll come." We head to class.

Lunchtime comes quickly and I head to our normal table where Josie and Marisol are already sitting. "Hi girls! Have you picked out your clothes for tonight? My dad got me a great dress. I can't wait." I look up and see Ruby walk into the cafeteria, but she isn't heading our way.

Josie jumps up and dashes to her, leading her to our table. I explain to Ruby that I am willing to forgive her and she can come with us in the limo to the dance.

Her response dumbfounds me! Ruby goes on about Rebeccah, telling me *I was wrong* and *I was mean!*

What? I start to tell her that she has no sense of humor and *she's* the bad friend, but she is already walking away from the table. I feel the blood rush to my face. I am mad and embarrassed.

"Can you believe her?" I say to Marisol and Josie?

"Actually," Josie says quietly, "I kind of agree with her."

Marisol adds, "It was kind of mean, Penelope."

I look at them in disbelief and mumble, "Whatever."

After an uncomfortable silence, Josie changes the subject and says, "Hey, are you guys ready for the test next week in health?" I don't respond.

The rest of the afternoon creeps along, and I can't concentrate. I don't want to go to this stupid dance now. I keep reviewing what Ruby said to me and my stomach hurts. Did I do something wrong? I thought it was all in good fun, but now I'm not sure. It doesn't feel funny anymore.

When I get home, Melinda stops her yoga and says, "Your mom called for you. She wants to FaceTime with you before the dance."

For the first time that day I feel excited. I really miss Mom, especially when she's been away. It's hard enough that I stay mostly with my dad, but they've both explained that, given

Mom's situation, it makes living with her too difficult. I call her back, keeping my fingers crossed that she's available. I'm relieved when I hear her voice.

"Hi honey," she says, "how's my girl?"

I surprise myself by sobbing into the phone. She asks what's wrong, and I ramble about the situation with Ruby. I don't tell her exactly what happened, but I feel like she is sympathetic and supportive, which makes me cry more. When we get off the phone, I think more about my friendship with Ruby and realize that, maybe, she's right. What I did to Rebeccah wasn't nice. Is it too late to make it right? I decide to talk to them at the dance.

Rebeccah

The Flake Finale

Friday Night

Finally, you get to hear from me, Rebeccah. You've probably learned a little about me already but to summarize, I live with my parents and I'm basically a happy person. I will say, however, I'm a little shy.

It's been a hard two weeks so I'm a little nervous when Ruby picks me up for pizza. I feel relieved that she and I are on better terms, but I'm still embarrassed by what happened. I keep telling myself, "Act like you own the place." That's what my dad always says to me when I don't feel comfortable. He also reminded me that, if I want to come home, I can call him. We have a code word in our family when things aren't going well. I'm excited to hang out with Ben, Elías, and the other guys. I don't really know them that well, but Elías is really nice and Ben is cute!

When we arrive at Pizza Palace, it's really busy. I quickly scan the room to see if anyone I don't want to see is here. I'm especially nervous about running into Jason. I thought he was cute, but, after Penelope's little stunt, I realized he's not exactly a nice guy. I feel my face getting hot just thinking about it. Ruby seems confident as she walks over to the guys and starts chatting. I wish I could be that comfortable. The guys say "hi" and we find a seat at the back of the restaurant.

Tonight is going great. I started out nervous, but now feel relaxed. Ruby and the guys are lots of fun. Maybe I was a little hard on Ruby, but I was so embarrassed. I do think she is a good friend and we all make mistakes. Later, Isaac asks Ruby and me if we're ready to head to The Flake. Ruby looks at me and shrugs, I surprise myself by saying yes.

When we arrive, the dance is in full force. Isaac and Elías put their cookies on the table. Isaac's are green and look a little creepy. He jokes they're made from the mold in science lab.

Elías offers chocolate chip cookies to us and says, "Here,

have some of these ... at least you know what these will taste like!"

At that moment, Jason and his friends walk to the table. He says, "Thanks for the cookies, loser." He grabs the tray of cookies and turns to me. "Hi, Rebeccah," he taunts, "how are you?" He gives me a smug smile.

I feel like melting into the ground. Ruby puts her arm protectively around me, "She's fine Jason. Don't you have something better to do? Those cookies aren't yours, by the way."

"Oh yeah," Jason replies. "What are you going to do about it? Is your little nerd friend going to stop me?" Holding the tray in one hand, he turns toward Elías and shoves two fingers into his chest.

I feel really anxious and fight the urge to run.

Suddenly, Penelope steps up. "You better give those back, Jason Thomas!"

Jason looks at her and rolls his eyes. "What's your deal? It's not like you care about the dork crew or Rebeccah goody-good."

"Actually, Jason—even though it's hard for me to say—I was wrong."

Jason looks taken aback as he drops the cookies onto the
table. He steps back, bumps into one of his buddies, who trips
on the skirt of the tablecloth and falls forward. Things seem to
go in slow motion as the table pitches over and cookies and
punch go flying.

"Watch out!" Penelope yells as the ladle filled with punch

flies through the air. The ladle crashes onto Jason's head, spilling red punch down his face and shirt.

At that exact moment, the song ends, and it's dead silent in the room. "What the heck!" screams Jason. He stomps his foot and looks like he's going to have a tantrum. The whole room is looking at him. Jason suddenly notices everyone is staring and makes a quick exit out of the room.

Ben bends down and picks a green cookie off the floor, blows on it, and says, "The fifteen-second rule." He takes a bite and says matter-of-factly, "Hey, these Franken-cookies aren't so bad!" The tension breaks and everyone laughs.

We move out of the way so the custodian and chaperones can salvage what they can and clean up the mess.

Penelope looks solemn and tells me, "I'm really sorry Rebeccah." She turns toward Ruby and says, "Ruby, I owe you an apology, too."

"Thanks for saying that, Penelope. Apology accepted," I say.

"Yeah, it means a lot," adds Ruby.

Even though Penelope apologized, it's going to take me a while to trust her. She was pretty mean, but this is a step in the right direction. Penelope grabs Ruby's and my arms and says,

"Come on girls, let's go have fun!" Marisol and Josie look relieved and everyone heads to the dance floor. The music starts and I notice Elías heading towards Ruby.

Tonight is turning into a great night. *I feel like I own the place!*

Companion Guide

Here's How to Deal: Dance Dilemma

The following questions can be used as a guide when thinking about the events of each chapter. Discuss, think about, or write your answers down.

Chapter One: Mold and Homework—
Not a Winning Combo!

1. What do you think? Should Ben cheat off his friend?

2. What do you think will happen if he does (in terms of the school and his friendship with Elías?)

3. What do you think the school's reaction might be?

4. What might Ben's parent's say?

5. How might Ben feel if he cheats?

6. Can you think of other choices he might make?

Chapter Two: To Flake or Flake Out

1. What do you think? How do you think Elías feels?

2. Do you think Elías made the right decision to not cover for his friend? Why or why not?

3. Elías made a choice not to cover for Ben. What if Elías made a different choice? What might the outcomes have been?

Chapter Three: Distraction and Drama

1. How do you think Rebeccah feels?

2. How do you think Ruby feels?

3. Why won't Rebeccah talk to Ruby?

4. Should Ruby say anything to Penelope now?

5. Do you think Ruby is responsible for what happened? Could she have prevented this?

6. What could she say to Rebeccah?

7. Is saying something to or about someone on the computer the same or different as saying something to or about someone in person?

8. How do you think social media sites can help or hurt friends?

9. How would you help friends in this situation?

Chapter Four: Dressed to Impress

1. What prompts Penelope to be critical of Ruby?

2. What do you think about Penelope's choice to send the text to Jason and his friends?

3. Why would she want to embarrass Rebeccah?

4. How do you think Penelope feels now that she has made that choice?

Chapter Five: Truth and Consequences

1. Ben gets the consequence of detention for his decision to cheat. Do you think he deserved that consequence?

2. Ben and Elías both liked Ruby. Has this ever happened to you? How would you feel?

3. What prompts Ben and Elías to make up?

Chapter Six: Don't Flake on a Friendship

1. What are things that Elías and Ben think are important to friendship?

2. Elías appears to have very set opinions about what is right or wrong in a friendship. Do you think there is ever an in between?

3. Elías is disappointed in Ruby because she did not stand up for Rebeccah, but why does he decide to help Ruby in class?

4. Why does Elías decide to forgive Ben? How would you have worked it out with your friends?

5. What did you think of how Ben defended Elías? How would you have defended or helped a friend in a similar situation?

6. What do you think Ben and Elías have learned about friend-ship? Is there anything else that they need to resolve?

Chapter Seven: Left Out and Limo-less

1. Why does Ruby feel conflicted about her friendship with Penelope?

2. Do you think Ruby is afraid of Penelope? Why or why not?

3. Why does she feel sorry for Penelope?

4. Why do you think Rebeccah refuses to accept Ruby's note?

5. Ruby's mom has a conversation with Ruby about her situation. If this happened to you, how would you apologize? What would a good friend do? How would you handle the situation if one of your friends hurt another friend?

6. Who are two adults you would talk to if you had a problem?

7. What is an advocate? What is an ally?

Chapter Eight: Perfect Dress

1. How does Penelope feel about her friendship with Ruby?

2. How do you think she defines "being a good friend?"

3. Do you think she feels conflicted?

4. Why does Penelope ask herself why she is "not more excited?"

5. If you were to write a journal entry for Penelope that showed her true inner emotions, what might she say? What might she be feeling?

About the Authors

Drs. Eleanor Gil-Kashiwabara, Shayna Brody Whitehouse and Erika Q. Laing are 3 Docs Press. These three friends found themselves in thoughtful and complex conversations about the challenges and everyday life experiences their children (and their children's peers), were facing. As well, they noticed a gap in the literature for the middle school age group related to social and emotional learning. Inspired by their collective experiences as psychologists and as moms, 3 Docs Press was born.

Dr. Gil-Kashiwabara is a Research Associate Professor at Portland State University and has focused her professional work around culturally appropriate mental health service for children and families, including those of Latina/o and American Indian/ Alaska Native backgrounds. She lives in Portland, Oregon with her family, including two daughters, ages 6 and 12. In her free time she enjoys yoga, dancing and running.

Dr. Brody Whitehouse lives with her family, including her two sons (a teen and tween), in the greater Boulder Colorado area. Her professional background is in school psychology and she has worked in the schools, in private practice and as a professor in a school psychology graduate program. She can be found skiing and hiking during her free time.

Dr. Q. Laing lives in Lafayette, Colorado with her family, including her two sons. Her professional background as a psychologist ranges the age span from very young to geriatrics and she has worked in private practice, group and hospital settings. During her leisure time, Dr. Q. Laing enjoys hiking, reading, writing and creating art of any kind.

All are excited to be part of this collaboration and hope that this book and the series will promote valuable conversations between adults and kids.